A souvenir guide

Stourhead

Wiltshire

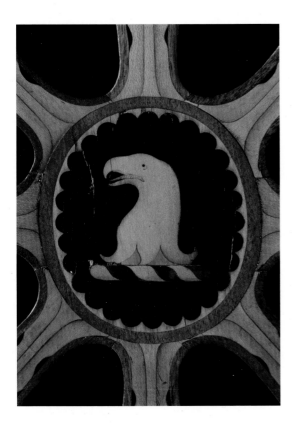

50p

M000111140

National Trust

Planting Paradise

Stourhead, a sublime landscape garden, is the creation of one family who, almost 300 years ago, built a mansion designed by Colen Campbell in the Wiltshire countryside and began to create their paradise here.

'We reached Stourhead at 3 o'clock. By that time the sun had penetrated the mist, and was gauzy and humid… Never do I remember such Claude-like, idyllic beauty here. See Stourhead and die.'

James Lees-Milne, May 1947

A family blessed and cursed

The Hoares, goldsmiths-turned-bankers, were blessed and cursed in equal measure, amassing a fortune through their private bank, C. Hoare & Co., in the City of London, and achieving great status in society. But each generation suffered family tragedy through the deaths of beloved wives and children, often through childbirth. Many Hoare fathers outlived their offspring. Only twice, through the seven generations who inherited the estate, did Stourhead pass from father to son. But they were a large and close family, and those who inherited fell under Stourhead's spell.

The approach

Today a modern bridge over the village road gives a glimpse of the ancient castellated gatehouse, moved by Richard Colt Hoare to mark the winding drive to the family's fine eighteenth-century villa. Before approaching the house, there is the restored Walled Garden where fruit and vegetables are still grown. In the lower walled garden is a dipping pond where the gardeners employed by the Hoare family would have filled their heavy metal watering-cans, or manually pumped the water, as they tended the produce for the table. It is here too that the Pelargonium House, a restored Victorian greenhouse, holds an excellent selection of tender pelargoniums in memory of Colt Hoare, who collected and bred these lovely plants.

Walk up the driveway, lined on the right with ancient sweet chestnut trees, past the old stable yard to the elegant Palladian-style house. Climb the portico steps before turning to look at the wide view over ancient farmland and the Iron Age hill fort of Whitesheet Hill.

Opposite A classic view: the Pantheon from across the lake

Below The east entrance front of the house

Entrance Hall

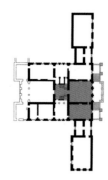

Above **The gilt bust of Charles I; by Hubert Le Sueur (c.1580–after 1658)**

Left **The Entrance Hall**

The Entrance Hall was designed to welcome, to impress and to be practical: hence the marble floor, which was originally flagstone and the robust hall-chairs. The room was gutted by fire in 1902, and the early eighteenth-century plasterwork decoration had to be remade by Edwardian craftsmen.

Pictures

Here hang portraits of the main cast of characters, timeless in oil on canvas.

Here you'll find Henry 'the Good', who bought the property in 1717 and built his grand country house. Henry, straight-backed and bewigged, white lace ruffs at his wrists, slender fingers carefully outlined, holds a half-rolled architectural drawing in his right hand. It is the design for his new house. And here too is his son, Henry 'the Magnificent', sitting resplendent, booted and spurred, deep in the saddle of a magnificent grey horse. The horse rears gently but his rider clearly holds no fear of being unseated. A massive classical column, trees, a hard, red foreign soil, a stretch of water, a small heap of tumbled stones and a sky suffused with light breaking through marbled clouds – all speak of classical Italy, the land that inspired this Henry to build his garden at Stourhead.

Facing Henry 'the Magnificent', across the green- and white-tiled floor, is the black-clad figure of his grandson, Richard Colt Hoare, sad-eyed and clutching a portfolio of drawings. Holding his arm is his young son, Henry. Again the background is classical, for it was Colt Hoare, archaeologist, antiquarian and passionate improver of the gardens and house at Stourhead, who cared for his grandfather's creation and secured its future.

Sculpture

The gilt-bronze sculpture of *Charles I* was made about 1635 by the French sculptor Hubert Le Sueur. It left the royal art collection in 1650 after the king's execution and has been at Stourhead since the mid-eighteenth century.

Inner Hall

The original staircase was destroyed in the 1902 fire, and was replaced by the present double flights and galleries.

Music Room

The room takes its name from the chamber organ that Henry Hoare 'the Magnificent' installed in the niche opposite the fireplace, but which was destroyed in the fire.

Furniture

The furniture is a mixture of Chippendale pieces made specially for the house and items introduced from other Hoare family houses such as Wavendon in Buckinghamshire.

Pictures

The paintings were bought mostly by Colt Hoare, who described them as 'a pleasing selection of fancy pictures, by modern Artists of the British School'.

Library

This is one of the finest surviving Regency library in Britain. It was built in 1792 by Messrs Moulton & Atkinson of Salisbury, and it seems very probable that Colt Hoare was closely involved in its design. A watercolour by Francis Nicholson (1753–1844) shows Colt Hoare at work in his beloved Library.

Pictures

The Library's barrel ceiling, decorated simply with a lattice-work design, is finished at the inner end with a canvas fitting the space between the wall and the curve of the ceiling. Samuel Woodforde was commissioned to paint *Apollo and the Nine Muses* shown promoting artistic creativity. The scene is echoed at the far end with a window, painted by Francis Eginton (1737–1805) after Raphael's Vatican fresco *The School of Athens,* again depicting great thinkers.

Furniture

During his remodelling of the house, Colt Hoare commissioned Thomas Chippendale the Younger to furnish Stourhead. Chippendale went bankrupt in 1804, and it was only thanks to the loyalty of a few clients like Colt Hoare that he managed to rebuild the business and continue until his death in 1822.

Far left John Milton as a young man; by John Michael Rysbrack

Left A modern portrait reputedly of Thomas Chippendale the Younger (1749–1822) not in the Stourhead collection and owned by the Chippendale Society

Below Thomas Chippendale the Younger's library furniture is decorated with Egyptian motifs, which were fashionable in the early nineteenth century

Books

Colt Hoare assembled a vast library of rare volumes on the history and topography of Britain, largely to provide source material for his scholarly publications, *The Ancient History of Wiltshire* (1810–21) and *The History of Modern Wiltshire* (1822–44). Unfortunately, most of Colt Hoare's books were sold in 1883, but some of his manuscripts and travel journals survive. Colt Hoare's archaeological collection is now in the Wiltshire Museum, Devizes. The Library today is a miscellany from Wavendon and Oxenham, the family estate in Devon.

Little Dining Room
South Apartments
Saloon

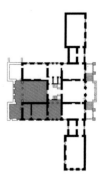

Little Dining Room

The Little Dining Room began life as a garden
hall, providing access to the south lawn
outside, down twin flights of steps. But when
Colt Hoare added the Library wing in 1792, he
removed the door to the garden and the steps.
Between 1802 and 1809 he renovated the room
and bought new furniture from Chippendale.
The name 'Little Dining Room' was introduced
in Victorian times to distinguish the room from
the Saloon, used as a large dining room for
more formal occasions.

Silver

The great silver-gilt dish on the mahogany
sideboard is a reminder that the family's
banking house grew out of their seventeenth-
century goldsmith's business. The dish, made

in Augsburg, the centre of European goldsmithing, was given to Sir Richard Hoare, Colt Hoare's grandfather, when he became Lord Mayor of London in 1745. Another reminder of the family's background is the showy seventeenth-century silver-gilt and agate salt cellar. It takes the form of a double-headed eagle, the family emblem.

Furniture

Other essential pieces of furniture for any dining room include the large oval wine-cooler and the mahogany sideboard and side-table by Thomas Chippendale the Younger, fitted with a customary cupboard for a chamberpot for the use of gentlemen after the ladies withdrew.

Pictures

In *Modern Wiltshire,* Colt Hoare describes the pastel portraits as being in 'a style now quite unfashionable'. However, they illustrate perfectly the Hoare family's long-standing and continuing interest in classical antiquity. Henry 'the Magnificent' had also been on a grand tour and commissioned William Hoare of Bath (*c.*1707–92) to produce these portraits of his relatives dressed as characters from Roman legends. William Hoare was not related to the banking Hoares until his daughter, Mary, also a fine artist, married 'Fat Harry' Hoare (uncle of Richard Colt Hoare and nephew to Henry 'the Magnificent') in 1765.

There are also pastel portraits by Francis Cotes (1726–70) of Sir Richard Hoare, 1st Baronet, who married Anne, the daughter of his uncle, Henry Hoare 'the Magnificent'. Anne (known as Nanny), also portrayed, died soon after her son, Richard Colt, was born. Richard's second wife, Frances Ann Acland, is part of this family group too.

South Apartments

These have always been the private family quarters and are still used and lived in by a member of the Hoare family today.

Saloon

Although originally intended as a chapel, this room was used by Henry Hoare 'the Magnificent' as a grand reception room, in which he could host county balls and other formal entertainments, and also as the setting for large dinner parties. The 1902 fire destroyed the room, which was rebuilt with a lower ceiling so that bedrooms could be added above. The screen of columns was inspired by those in the Little Dining Room.

Pictures

In keeping with the room's Edwardian atmosphere, it is hung with portraits and 'fancy' pictures by St George Hare, an artist much patronised by Alda, Lady Hoare.

Above **The Saloon**

Opposite left The late seventeenth-century silver-gilt dish was made by Heinrich Mannlich and is displayed in a stand possibly by Sefferin Alken

Opposite right The Little Dining Room

Column Room
Italian Room
Cabinet Room

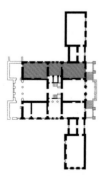

Column Room

Colt Hoare hung watercolours in this room, which had been a 'bedchamber with columns' in 1762. Today it still displays large watercolours, of Rome and the surrounding countryside, by the Swiss artist Abraham-Louis Ducros (1748–1810), whose style of painting Colt Hoare believed would have an important influence on English artists.

Italian Room

The Italian Room was conceived by Henry 'the Good' as a state bedroom, although by 1720 the royal court was much more static than it had been in Tudor times, and the convention of reserving a bed for visiting royalty had ended.

Colt Hoare used the Italian Room as his own bedroom, installing a 'four post bedstead [with] Mahogany feet pillars and Chintz furniture.'

Right The elegant mid-eighteenth-century marble chimneypiece was brought from Wavendon and incorporates a plaque representing *The marriage of Cupid and Psyche*. The figures in the overmantel painting, *The Sacrifice of Iphigenia*, are by Jacopo Amigoni (?1682–1752) and the capriccio of buildings in antique Rome and Glanum (now Saint-Rémy-de-Provence) is by Francis Hardman (active 1745–67)

Left The Cabinet Room

Below The Pope's Cabinet is displayed in its niche. Mrs Lybbe Powis recorded in 1776 that 'in the third room shown is the so-much-talked-of cabinet that once belong'd to Pope Sixtus, which Mr Hoare purchased at an immense sum, so great that he says he will never declare the sum.'

Cabinet Room

One of the most treasured possessions of Henry 'the Magnificent' sits in splendour in the Cabinet Room, named for his extraordinary Roman cabinet, glittering with gilt-bronze mounts, semi-precious stones and elaborate architectural ornament. The *pietra dura* cabinet was brought to Stourhead by Henry who acquired it in Rome during his Grand Tour as having been made for Pope Sixtus V whose papacy, from 1585 to 1590, coincided with the Spanish Armada. Recent research has confirmed its provenance. Constructed of pine with a thin layer of African black wood to resemble ebony, its superb quality became apparent during restoration in 2006–7 when two of over 150 more-or-less secret drawers could not be opened.

Colt Hoare refurnished the Cabinet Room in 1802. The textiles he purchased have long since perished and are known only from

Chippendale's accounts: a green serge floor cloth, 'blue Rosette callico' cushion covers, a Sattin window curtain of blue with black spots, a pair of footstools in red Morocco leather, and, most sumptuous of all, a curtain for the alcove of 'Rich blue velvet' with a gold fringe and tassels. The decorative scheme was designed to show off the Pope's Cabinet and ensure it had pride of place in the room.

Chippendale was later commissioned to create an ornate gilt cornice for the niche curtain, 'finished in Burnished Gold with the Pope's tiara and other insignias'. (The cornice was destroyed in the fire, but the cabinet was rescued.) Partly concealed by the blue velvet curtain, the cabinet would have gleamed in the semi-darkness like some great shrouded reliquary. The Cabinet Room was one of the rooms opened by Colt Hoare to visitors, and was described by him in the first guidebook, published in the early nineteenth century.

Picture Gallery

Whilst travelling on the Continent, both Henry 'the Magnificent' and Richard Colt Hoare commissioned and collected numerous works of art and shipped them back to Stourhead. Having decided that the house was too small for his needs, Colt Hoare constructed the Library and Picture Gallery, and the building of the north wing was completed in 1802. Inspired by the picture galleries he had seen in Italy, he gathered together the pick of his grandfather's collection and of his own Old Masters and contemporary paintings.

Above The Picture Gallery, lit by three east-facing windows

Furniture

The Picture Gallery was intended as a formal room where the shutters were closed and furniture shrouded in case covers (supplied by Chippendale), except when Colt Hoare was showing the collection to visitors.

Chippendale supplied all the original furnishings for the Picture Gallery, including a fitted Brussels carpet, 'Yellow and black star sattin' curtains and chair cushions in 'Yellow Star callico'. These yellow textiles, the satinwood and ebony furniture and the gilt picture frames would have made a dazzling decorative scheme.

Pictures

Many of the paintings collected by Henry and his grandson, Colt Hoare, were sold in the late nineteenth century. But three massive paintings still hang exactly where Colt Hoare placed them when the Gallery was complete.

His prized *Adoration of the Magi* by Ludovico Cardi (Il Cigoli) (1559–1613), with its magnificent ornate frame, carved by Thomas Chippendale, is in prime position over the mantelpiece, flanked by his grandfather's *Caesar and Cleopatra* by Adolf Mengs (1728–79) and *Marchese Pallavicini and the Artist* by Carlo Maratta (1625–1713).

Henry's *The Choice of Hercules* by Nicolas Poussin (1594–1665) escaped the auctioneer's hammer in the sale of 1883 and hangs on the Picture Gallery's entrance wall.

Colt Hoare was also a patron of contemporary English artists. He was especially moved by female distress. In 1806 he bought *Distress by Sea* by Henry Thomson (1773–1843) and in 1811 its companion, *Distress by Land*. In *Modern Wiltshire*, he writes: 'These two admirable specimens of the modern school of painting, they speak to the eyes as to good colouring and composition and to the feeling heart as to the expressions and distressful situations of the unhappy sufferers.'

Distress by Land has all the sublime ingredients, drama and pathos to appeal to his sympathy. A young girl clutching an infant to her breast, whilst sheltering a small boy in her cloak, is struggling against thunder, lightning and rain on a bleak Salisbury plain. The backdrop of Stonehenge adds an extra dimension to the scene, which must have appealed to Colt Hoare's antiquarian interests.

Above A corner of the fire-surround

Left *The Adoration of the Magi*; by Ludovico Cardi (Il Cigoli), 1605

What Is a Landscape Garden?

At least a decade before that best-known advocate of the English 'landscape garden', Lancelot 'Capability' Brown tore down the barriers between the grand country house and its surrounding park, private landowners were making gardens inspired by the idea of a landscape influenced by art.

Turning their backs on the formal, geometric layouts of previous generations, they set to work on their acres of meadow and woodland with a painterly eye, rather than a plumb line and protractor, to improve the scene before them.

Influences on design

Many landowners, often newly wealthy men, made the 'Grand Tour' of Europe, soaking up the classical atmosphere engendered by the profusion of 'antiquities' they discovered, especially in Italy. Many returned with statues and architectural remains that spoke of a glorious past that could be recreated at home.

These landed gentry, educated and well-read, had a reverence, not only for their God and the glorious nature created by the deity, but also for the artists who portrayed that nature in all its simple beauty. They wanted to have and to hold a picture that would please not only the eye, but also the enquiring mind, pointing a way to the future by drawing on the lessons of the past.

Their imaginations were fired by writers such as Joseph Addison, who advocated a middle way between the expensively controlled European landscape gardens, where extreme formality gradually ceded to meadows and woods, and the traditional English park, filled with deer for the chase.

Why not, he wrote, use what you already have? Why not use the 'natural embroidery of the meadows' by improving the paths between and adding some pieces of 'art'?

Landscape architect William Kent began to work by eye in the early eighteenth century, 'arranging' the landscape by the use of shape, size, light and shade and contrasting colours. His work at Stowe in Buckinghamshire became famous, as did the landscaping of Painshill Park in Surrey by its owner, the Hon. Charles Hamilton. Hamilton was well known to the Hoare family and borrowed £6,000 from Hoare's bank to finance his creation.

The other major influence on these gentlemen was the work of romantic landscape painters, such as the Baroque paintings and engravings of the seventeenth-century artists Claude Lorrain, Nicolas Poussin and Poussin's brother-in-law, Gaspar Dughet. The Hoare family admired and possessed paintings by all three men.

As the spirit moved him

It was only after Susannah, the wife of Henry Hoare 'the Magnificent' died in 1743, leaving him to care for their three children, that he began his great work. Working *'con spirito'* (as the spirit moved him) in the words of his grandson, Richard Colt Hoare, he started to create his famous garden.

Left The Palladian Bridge at Stowe, one of the great eighteenth-century landscape gardens. The bridge was completed in 1738

Left Gaspard Dughet's *Classical Landscape* of c.1658–9 was one of the paintings in the collection of Henry Hoare 'the Magnificent' that inspired his garden

An inspired adviser

Henry Hoare's chief partner, adviser and designer in his grand vision for Stourhead was the talented architect Henry Flitcroft, a close colleague of William Kent and Lord Burlington.

Henry could not have completed his building programme without Flitcroft, but he seems to have relied on his own judgement when planting the 'naked hills and dreary valleys', in the words of an early visitor, with trees and shrubs. A team of 50 gardeners, supervised by Henry's steward Francis Faugoin, planted and tended beech, oak, sycamore, Spanish chestnut, ash and holm oak. Yew trees were planted, as were larch, spruce and cedar. Henry insisted that the plantings create a pleasing picture: 'The greens should be ranged together in large masses as the shades are in painting: to contrast the dark masses with *light* ones, and to relieve each dark mass itself with little sprinklings of lighter greens here and there.'

A happy accident

Flitcroft's rise to prominence in the architectural field came about by sheer chance. A fall from the scaffolding at Burlington House, where he was working as a carpenter, resulted in a broken leg.

While he was laid up, he spent his time drawing and his designs and pictures were noticed by the 'architect Earl', Lord Burlington, who soon employed him as his draughtsman and general architectural assistant, providing the inspiration which he in turn brought to Stourhead.

Right The architect Henry Flitcroft (1697–1769), who had a key role in creating the Stourhead landscape garden

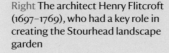

Making the lake

Henry Hoare 'the Magnificent' was one of a small group of early eighteenth-century 'gentlemen gardeners' using their acres to create a particularly personal landscape which expressed their hopes and beliefs about the world and their journey through it. His vision, recreating a classical landscape, depended on water.

Henry Hoare dammed the valley to create the lakes that are the key to the garden

The centrepiece of the garden at Stourhead is the lake. This expanse of water, on which dragonflies dance, swallows swoop and crested grebes swim together in their strange mating ritual, brings life to the picture. The reflection of trees in the water, the movement as wind brushes the surface, the small sounds of waves lapping the banks, entice all the senses as you embark on the journey around Henry Hoare's paradise. The lake also dictates the path you take and the views you enjoy.

The damming of the river and the creation of the lake, which was formed from the two existing fish-ponds, was an ambitious undertaking. Henry and his architect, Henry Flitcroft, planned it before work began on the garden buildings, but these had to be constructed before the water level could be altered. It was understood that a retaining stone border must be in place the whole way around the lake before the dam was built and the low ground flooded. This eventually happened in 1755.

Clues to the sequence of work come from letters between Flitcroft and his employer and from the banker's personal ledgers, where his accounts for the house and gardens at Stourhead are kept in minute detail.

The first letters from Flitcroft are dated 1744, when he mentions the 'Temple of Ceres' and the 'Rocky Arch in which I propose to place the River God'. He also bravely writes of planning

his suggestions for the dam or 'how I conceive the head of the lake should be formed'. He reassures Henry 'Twill make a most agreeable scene, with the solemn shade about it...'

The letters and the accounts show work continuing apace until 1751, when there is a gap of almost two years. The reason is not spelled out, but it was in 1752 that Henry's only son, also Henry, died in Naples at the age of 21. This was a devastating blow to a man who had lost his two wives. He tried to bear his sorrow with fortitude, writing to his brother, Richard: 'I have been taught by our Holy Religion, and by former visitations, tryals and afflictions to submit myself before the throne of God who...still supports me under a grief I never expected or wished to have survived.'

But, two years later, in 1753, his elder daughter Susanna (Sukey) was married and Henry was making arrangements for the marriage of Anne (Nanny), his younger daughter, to her cousin, Richard Hoare. Records show that this was the year that he planned to build the greatest and most impressive 'temple' at Stourhead – the iconic Pantheon.

Above The statue of a classical River God faces the exit from the Grotto and suggests the route to the Pantheon

Below The path through the woods around the lake was designed to be taken in an anti-clockwise direction

Enchanting paths
Letters to his nephew and future son-in-law, Richard Hoare, at this time, show Henry characteristically philosophising over the acquisition of the 'enchanting paths of Paradise'. 'Those are the fruits of industry and application to business and shows what great things may be done by it, the envy of the indolent who have no claim to Temples, Grottos, Bridges, Rocks, Exotick Pines, and Ice in summer,' he wrote.

A walk around the lake

Most early visitors would have seen the house first, before following the path across the lawn and descending gently to the first glimpse of what lies below. There, to the left, is the church – a reminder of the end of all our journeys.

Ice House

Tucked away in the trees off the house lawn is the Ice House, that luxury afforded only to the rich in the days before refrigeration. A short passage into the domed building leads to the brick-lined central chamber where great chunks of ice, cut from the frozen lake in winter, would be stored between insulating layers of straw and kept for use in the kitchen in summer. Henry

'the Magnificent', writing to his nephew and son-in-law Richard Hoare, pointed out that hard work, 'fruits of industry and application to business', brought about such good things as 'ice in summer'. The Ice House was restored by the Trust in 1983.

Fir Walk

To the right is the grassy path through the Fir Walk, brought to a full stop by the Obelisk, an Egyptian symbol of the ever-shining sun. First built in 1746, it was subsequently restored twice as it crumbled in the nineteenth century, only to be struck by lightning in 1853. The walk to the obelisk was the original, circuit walk from the house.

Above The Temple of Flora, formerly called the Temple of Ceres, has a single room and a portico of Tuscan Doric order columns

Temple of Flora

The higher path will take you behind the Temple of Flora, the first garden building, built purposely above a spring. There is a steepish path, zig-zagging down through the trees which allows a closer look at the temple, dedicated to the Roman goddess of fertility, flowers and spring. The best view is to be had when you reach the Pantheon, on the opposite bank, and look back across the widest part of the lake.

Both Henry 'the Magnificent' and his successor, his grandson Richard Colt Hoare, viewed the Pantheon as the climax of the journey, teasing and tempting the visitor on the path as now it comes into view before you twist away to lose it again.

Today the path extends right around the lake but in the late eighteenth century the visitor crossed the water, first by a long wooden Chinese Bridge which reached close to the Grotto on the north side, passing behind the little island. It was later replaced by a rowing boat serving as a ferry because the bridge had fallen into disrepair.

Six Wells Bottom

The path turns back on itself between Lily Lake and a dark pool known as Diana's Basin. It is here that the springs that flow into the lake, the 'Six Wells', rise. After crossing Lily Lake dam, a short walk to the right reveals St Peter's Pump in the valley, built in 1474 to help supply water to the city of Bristol. It stood next to St Peter's church in the city but was taken out of use and bought by Henry Hoare in 1768 as an apt reminder of the source of the River Stour which helped him to create his lake.

Left **The Fir Walk leads to the Obelisk**

Right **St Peter's Pump**

Above the door of the Temple of Flora is carved the inscription: *Procul, O procul este, profani*. This is Henry Hoare, using words from Virgil's *Aeneid*, asking you to enter his garden in the right spirit. It was the warning spoken to Aeneas as he descended into the underworld, Hades, to receive directions about the future of Rome. Roughly translated it means: *Keep away, oh, keep far away you who are profane!*

The Grotto

If the Pantheon is the lofty peak of Henry's classical scheme at Stourhead, the dark, damp and atmospheric Grotto, with its flowing spring, sleeping nymph, craggy rocks and sublime view across the water through a jagged window, must be the dramatic highlight.

Above the original, pedimented entrance to the Grotto is another inscription from Virgil's story of the Trojan Aeneas. Translated, it reads *within, fresh water and seats in the living rock, the home of the nymphs*, linking the Grotto to the cave of the nymphs in Carthage where Aeneas and the tragic Queen Dido fell in love. Aeneas, sternly reminded that his duty to the Gods lay in Italy, wrenched himself away. Dido killed herself.

That entrance has been covered by the dark winding passage, added in 1776. It has been argued that the imposing figure of the River God, in his cave over the spring, pointing visitors onward to their goal, the Pantheon, represents Tiber, the god of the Roman river. Tiber appeared to Aeneas in a dream, rising from his river with shady reeds covering his hair, to prophesy success and victory in the exiled Trojan's quest.

The River God and probably the Nymph were made by sculptor John Cheere, the nymph after a much-copied original of the 'sleeping Ariadne' in the Belvedere Garden of the Vatican in Rome. The inscription on the pavement in front of the nymph's pool is a translation, by Alexander

Nymph of the grot, these sacred springs I keep
And to the murmur of these waters sleep;
Ah spare my slumbers, gently tread the cave
And drink in silence or in silence lave.

Nymph of the grot these sacred springs I keep
And to the murmur of these waters sleep
Ah spare my slumbers gently tread the cave
And drink in silence or in silence lave

A Pope.

Pope, of a fifteenth-century poem. Here it celebrates the spring that gives rise to the water that is the focal point of the garden. The nymph, forever asleep, lies above a pool in her arched recess in the domed central space of the Grotto. The darkness of the entrance gives way to this high-ceilinged round chamber with natural light pouring in from above and from the 'window' looking over the lake. It is a peaceful and contemplative scene but, as you turn to continue your journey up the rugged steps, the urgency and power of the River God's gesture jolts you back into reality.

Gothic Cottage

Times and fashions change. By the end of the eighteenth century, men of taste were going for Gothic designs, inspired by the so-called 'gloomth' of Horace Walpole's 'little Gothic castle' at Strawberry Hill, with tomb-inspired furnishings.

The cottage, prettily rustic, was largely hidden by trees until 1806, when Richard Colt Hoare made it a prominent garden feature by adding the Gothic decoration and the seat and porch. Today the cosiness of the cottage serves to make us pause on the path before rounding the corner to be confronted by the first close-up view of the magnificent Pantheon, last glimpsed from the southern shore of the lake.

Opposite **The Grotto**

Opposite below **The inscription in the Grotto**

Below **The Gothic Cottage**

Henry Hoare 'the Magnificent' spent as much time as he could at Stourhead and loved to describe it to his daughter, Sukey, and his granddaughter Harriot. He confided his delight in the cooling properties of the 'grot' during the scorching summer of 1764: 'A souse in that delicious bath and grot, filld with fresh magic, is Asiatick luxury, and too much for mortals, or at least for subjects. Next I shall ride under the spreading beeches just beyond the Obelisk where we are sure of wind and shade...'

The Pantheon

This is the home of Hercules, the sculpture commissioned from Michael Rysbrack in 1747 and installed ten years later. Here he stands, the figure based on the famous Farnese Hercules moved in 1787 from Rome to Naples, where Henry is almost certain to have seen it. Hercules, weary after the last of his twelve labours, leans on his trusty club, his lion-skin draped over its head. He gets his real-life muscles and fine physique from Rysbrack's model, Jack Broughton, a London prize-fighter. Hercules's somewhat effete pose is of its time and was much admired – especially by Horace Walpole, who thought the sculpture 'an exquisite summary of his skill, knowledge and judgement'. The statues of Flora and St Susanna in the Pantheon are by Rysbrack too. There is a terracotta working model of Hercules in the Library, left to Henry by Rysbrack when he died in 1770.

Henry associated his labours in the City with those of the heroic Hercules. The Poussin painting, showing Hercules at the crossroads, choosing between Pleasure and Virtue (he chose the latter, of course), hangs in the Picture Gallery in the house.

The Pantheon, designed and built by Flitcroft in 1753–4, and the great moral hero, Hercules, were, to Henry's mind, a combination that made 'a pattern of perfection'.

The niches each side of the portico contain sculptures of the goddess Venus (the mother of mortal Aeneas) and Bacchus, the god of wine. Inside, keeping company with Hercules, are: St Susanna; the goddess Diana, the huntress; Flora, goddess of gardens; Livia Augusta, Virgil's patron; the Greek hero Meleager; and Isis, the mother goddess of Egypt, who was worshipped widely as a patron of nature and magic.

A clue to the practical use to which this building was put by the family is the grille in the wall behind Hercules, part of a heating system used when the room was laid up for supper parties and picnics.

Cascade

The cascade that falls into the lake below the dam was devised by two friends and regular visitors to Stourhead. William Hoare, the portrait painter, who was no relation to the banking Hoares (although his daughter, Mary, married into the family), and Coplestone Warre Bampfylde, landscape enthusiast, who had constructed a cascade at Hestercombe, his home near Taunton, worked together to create the waterfall for Henry in 1765. Bampfylde also made a series of valuable panoramic sketches of the garden in the 1770s.

Above Michael Rysbrack's statue of Hercules in the Pantheon

Left *The Choice of Hercules*; by Nicolas Poussin

Opposite The lake and Pantheon with portico of four Corinthian columns

Temple of Apollo

Flitcroft's last building for Henry was the circular temple dedicated to the sun god Apollo. The route to the temple embodies the famous 'choice of Hercules' – between a superficially easier level path and a more difficult, but ultimately more rewarding, climb. The diversion, through the rock arch and up the steep zig-zag path, is well worth it for the glorious views from the temple, built in 1765, high on a hill overlooking the lake from the western edge. Henry wanted to outdo William Chamber's Temple of the Sun at Kew which, like his own new building, was based on the celebrated Syrian temple at Baalbec. Sadly the domed roof of this impressive building gradually fell into disrepair, and the National Trust undertook a massive restoration project, unveiling the repaired structure in all its glory early in 2010. Timbers, hewn from Stourhead Estate wood, formed the basic structure for the new dome, which was covered with lead and given a moulded plaster ceiling with an image of Apollo's head, radiating the golden rays of the sun at its centre.

Left Temple of Apollo

Opposite left Palladian Bridge

Opposite right Bristol Cross

Palladian Bridge

Sometime before Flitcroft designed the Temple of Apollo, his last building for Stourhead before his death in 1769, the rock bridge across the Zeals road and the underpass that leads back to the lake were built, while, in 1762, Henry was able to write to his daughter, Sukey, that the Palladian Bridge 'was now about'. 'It is simple and plain,' he wrote, 'I took it from Palladio's bridge at Vicenza, 5 arches; and when you stand at the Pantheon the water will be seen thro the arches and it will look as if the river came down through the village and that this was the village bridge for publick use.'

Bristol Cross

The medieval Bristol Cross was another acquisition from the city where it had stood at the junction of the High Street and Broad Street before being taken to pieces. Six wagons were hired to move it to Stourhead in 1764, but it was not until the following year that an attempt was made to assemble it. Henry wrote to his son-in-law, Lord Bruce, husband to his daughter Sukey: 'The cross is now in hand and there are so many pieces that we must I believe employ Harriot to put it together as she is such an adept in joyning the map of the Countys of England'. Harriot was Sukey's daughter and Henry's beloved granddaughter, Henrietta, who was about ten years old at the time.

Visitors to Stourhead

By 1770, the landscape garden at Stourhead was receiving considerable attention and a constant flow of visitors.

Henry 'the Magnificent' planned two more buildings, both of which were completed in 1772. The first was an inn, where the ever-increasing number of visitors could be put up in comfort. The second, far less prosaic, was a magnificent tribute to King Alfred, 'the Founder of the English Monarchy and Liberty' in the words of Henry. It was to stand, not inside the gardens but two miles off, on Kingsettle Hill, where it would be a sizeable landmark, visible in all directions, to the glories of Stourhead.

Visiting and admiring the great houses and gardens of others was an increasingly popular pastime for the leisured classes in the eighteenth and nineteenth centuries. Stourhead, a showcase for the latest in architecture and art, and with a garden whose reputation made it a 'must-see' attraction, was top of many people's list.

One such visitor was Mrs Philip (Caroline) Lybbe Powys, who kept diaries and wrote letters, describing her many explorations for more than 50 years from 1762.

'We have some years wish'd to see Stourhead,' she wrote, noting that she, her husband and two others, travelling in two phaetons from Oxfordshire, set off in August, visiting Wilton House and William Beckford's Fonthill along the way.

It is interesting to read that her reaction to figures of English monarchs in the Bristol Cross, erected in 1764, just inside the gardens, were 'ornamented with red, blue and gilt clothing'. The diarist thought the original stone colour would have been easier on the eye or that if it were moved to 'an eminence' where it could be seen at a little distance, it might be less 'strikingly gaudy'.

But her impressions elsewhere are wholly favourable. '... all the buildings and plantations are the present owner's own doing, without any assistance but common workmen to plan or lay out the whole seven miles extent, nor could Brown [Lancelot 'Capability' Brown] have executed it with more taste and elegance.

'These were nothing more than naked hills and dreary valleys, which are now so beautifully adorn'd by art, assisting Nature with trees, her greatest ornament, where hills and water only were before,' she wrote.

She remarks that the position of the garden buildings here outshone those at the famous gardens at Stowe in Buckinghamshire because of the 'much more beautiful spots each here is erected on'.

Although life in the village of Stourton now revolves around the world-famous garden, the parish of Stourton with Gasper is an ancient one. More than 600 people lived in the village which was owned by the Stourton family from Saxon times. Several cottages that once lay between the church and the garden were demolished in 1812 by Richard Colt Hoare (see pp. 52–3) to create a more picturesque view.

Opposite The garden in 1813 (detail); watercolour by Francis Nicholson

Below The Spread Eagle Inn has been welcoming visitors since 1772

Accommodating visitors

The Stourton Inn (today known as the Spread Eagle) was, it seems, rarely empty. Caroline Lybbe Powys was unlucky in her overnight accommodation. 'We intended laying at the inn at Stourton, built by Mr Hoare..., but to our great mortification, when we got there at near ten o'clock, it was full and we oblig'd to go on to Meer [Mere], a shocking little town three miles off...' she wrote. But Stourhead more than made up for poor accommodation in Mere: '...and in the morning returned to Stourhead, which answered every difficulty we had met with the preceding evening, as both house and grounds are so vastly worth seeing,' is her happy conclusion to the visit.

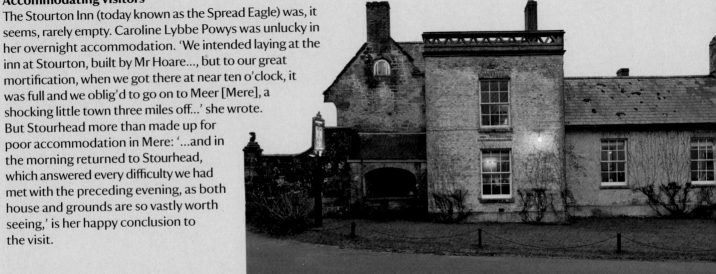

The Creators of Stourhead

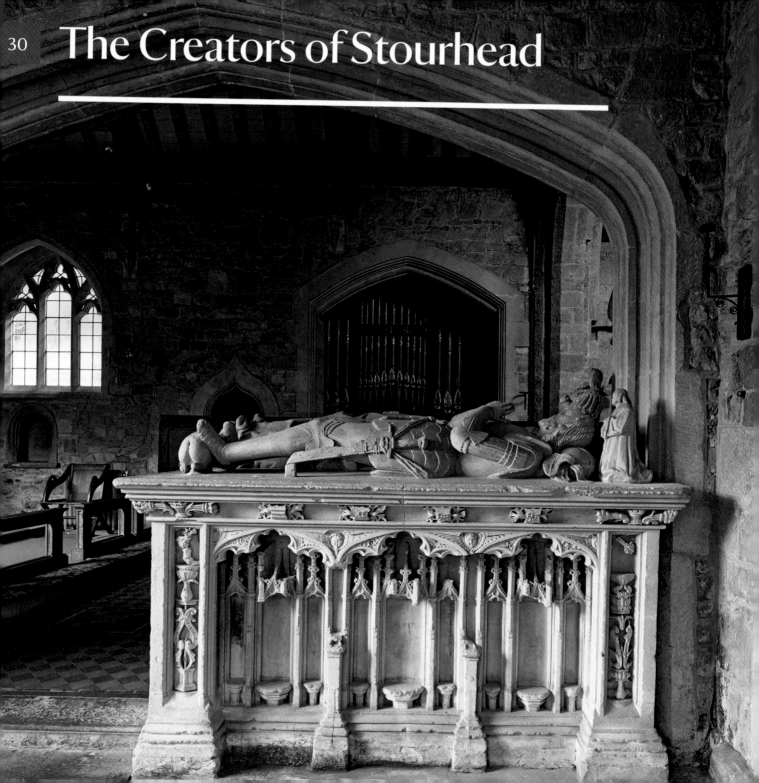

The Stourtons

Stourhead will forever be associated with the Hoare family, risen from the ranks of the merchant class to seek land to build their country mansions and to plough the wealth, earned by hard work and business acumen, into their newly acquired acres. But pay a visit to Stourton's thirteenth-century St Peter's church whose square tower plays counterpoint to the spire of the Hoares' Bristol Cross, and you'll see not only grand memorials to the Hoares – Henry 'the Good', 'the Magnificent' and Richard Colt Hoare – but also tomb effigies of members of a more ancient family, who had been lords of this piece of Wiltshire since Saxon times.

The medieval seat of the Stourtons, Stourton House, was demolished by the first Henry Hoare when he bought the ancient manor in 1717. The Stourton family had represented their people in Parliament for generations until Sir John Stourton, a favourite of the Plantagenet Henry VI, rose to become treasurer of the royal household and was made Baron Stourton in 1448, when he enlarged the house and grounds. He was granted a licence by the king to enclose a thousand acres of woodland, meadow and pasture, thus creating the first 'park' here.

At some time during the Stourtons' occupation, the River Stour, which rises in a valley below the present house, was dammed to made a series of fish-ponds. It is interesting that the family arms show 'six fountains', those 'fountains' being the springs that herald the source of the Stour in that valley which is still called Six Wells Bottom.

The Stourtons continued to prosper in the early reign of Henry VIII, owning land not only in Wiltshire, Dorset and Somerset, but also acquiring property in the south of England.

But fortunes changed, and scandal hit the family, who became impoverished and, on the Royalist and Catholic side in the Civil War, excluded from Parliament. Their estates, ransacked by Parliamentarians and encumbered by debt, were sold in the early eighteenth century, eventually passing to the Meres family and then to the Hoares, who were looking not only for a sound investment but also for an entrée into the ranks of the landed gentry.

Feuding families

Things began to go seriously wrong for the Stourtons in the latter part of the reign of Henry VIII. William, 7th Lord Stourton, left his wife, Elizabeth, and nine children at Kilmington, part of his estate, in the care of a tenant, William Hartgill. Lord Stourton, doing the King's work at Newhaven, lived openly with his mistress, Agnes Rhys, by whom he had one illegitimate daughter. When he died in 1548, he left nothing to his widow, although there was a considerable bequest to Agnes and the rest to his son, Charles, who succeeded him. Charles became embroiled in a feud with the Hartgill family over his mother's maintenance and the management of the estate. Matters came to a head in 1557, when he ordered the murder of Hartgill senior and his son. Charles and his four henchmen were tried and hanged in Salisbury Market Place on 6 March 1557.

Opposite The monument to the 5th Lord Stourton (d. 1546) in St Peter's church

Below St Peter's church, Stourton

At the sign of the Golden Bottle

Richard Hoare Kn.
Lord Mayor of the City
of London in the
Memorable Year
1746

It was new money that allowed Henry Hoare I to build his contemporary villa high on a Wiltshire hillside. The considerable amount required to finance his son's equally innovative landscape garden was not quite so new, but it came from the same source – the family bank, founded by Richard Hoare, father of Henry 'the Good', in 1672. The money was not easily earned, nor was it lightly spent. Richard Hoare, the only son of a reasonably prosperous horse-trader, served a long apprenticeship as a goldsmith, before buying his master's business and making it his own in 1673, a year after he was permitted to trade under his own name as a Freeman of the Worshipful Company of Goldsmiths.

Richard's determination to succeed and his unshakeable religious belief, combined with energy and natural integrity, helped him prosper in a business where many others, less acute than he, failed.

This work ethic was passed on to his sons, only four of whom survived him. Henry, his right-hand man in London, and Benjamin, the youngest brother, were both partners in the business, which, in 1690, moved to the premises in Fleet Street that the bank still occupies. Hanging from an ornamental bracket on the wall outside, high enough to allow a horse and rider to pass beneath, was a golden bottle. This served as the unique sign for the shop, in the days when visitors looked for symbols rather than door numbers.

The customers who borrowed or deposited money also brought their plate to be repaired or remade in a newer fashion, or bought luxury goods such as silver buttons, silver toothpicks, pepper boxes, sugar sifters, cups, tankards, porringers, teapots and cutlery. The craftsmen who worked for Richard Hoare were the best in London, and the customers who used banking services or 'the shop' – or both – included Samuel Pepys, Catherine of Braganza, Countess Fauconberg (daughter of Oliver Cromwell) and Richard 'Beau' Nash.

By 1702, when Henry, Richard's second son, was made a partner in the business, just over a third of the assets at the Golden Bottle related to the goldsmith's trade. Richard and his son still received orders for re-making or buying silverware and they kept a stock of gold, silver, diamonds and pearls for sale or to be used in making new pieces. But, by now, banking was the main thrust of the company. The Hoares, father and son, had weathered the creation, in 1694, of the Bank of England, although they had fought its establishment every inch of the way, fearing, as did other goldsmith-bankers, that it would put them out of business.

Richard helped to write a leaflet listing objections to this monolithic bank which was being created purely to manage the enormous public debt caused by William of Orange's wars against the French. He fretted that the new 'joint stock' bank would have a monopoly in lending and borrowing, thus driving out competition and bringing depression to the City of London. But, between them, Richard and Henry ensured that Hoare's survived – one of the very few to do so.

Richard, the former goldsmith's apprentice, made his mark when, in 1702, he was knighted by Queen Anne. This spurred him into becoming first an Alderman for the Bread Street ward of the City of London and then a Member of Parliament, with a host of honorary appointments. The climax of Richard Hoare's public career came in 1712, when he was made Lord Mayor of London.

Sir Richard, who died in January 1718, had seen his diligence, determination and reputation for integrity rewarded with high honour in the City. His son, Henry, was to establish the family name among the landed gentry throughout the country.

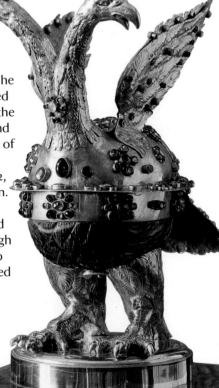

Opposite Sir Richard Hoare as Lord Mayor of London; painted by Jonathan Richardson the Elder about 1712 (detail)

Below A seventeenth-century silver-gilt centrepiece in the form of a double eagle, the Hoare family crest. The family made its fortune as goldsmiths before turning to banking

Henry 'the Good'

Richard Hoare had made his name in London and now it was the turn of his son, Henry, senior partner in the business on his father's death, to lead the family forward.

Henry had already been given the nickname 'The Good' by his friends, because of his generous founding and funding of charitable institutions, mainly hospitals and religious organisations.

But he knew that it was time to invest his money in a substantial property and, in doing so, to join the ranks of those with whom a great part of his business was done. An estate in the country would give him not only the political power that tracts of land conveyed, but also lend substance to the name of Hoare outside the city. He would join the ranks of the landed gentry, with the privilege and respect afforded to that class.

By the time he began to look for a suitable property, he had become a family man and, ever cautious not to over-commit himself, was aware that he would have to wait until he could separate his own income from that of the bank. The Hoares were a large and clannish family, and Henry had married his cousin Jane Benson when he became a partner in the bank in 1702.

He brought her home to the Golden Bottle in Fleet Street, where they lived with his parents, several bank clerks – and their four children, two of whom, Henry and Richard, would play a major part in the family story.

Sadly, seven other babies born to Jane and Henry in the first years of their marriage died before they reached their first birthdays.

Henry's quest for a country estate was made with the help of his wife's brother, William Benson, who succeeded Sir Christopher Wren as Surveyor-General (chief architect to the government). William was an enthusiastic promoter of the newly fashionable Palladian style of design, putting his ideas into practice in the building of his own property, Wilbury House, at Newton Toney in Wiltshire, also designed by Colen Campbell.

Henry greatly admired his brother-in-law's new villa, which was inspired by Amesbury Abbey – then believed to be by architect Inigo Jones, who had introduced this severely classical style of building to England a hundred years earlier. He resolved to search for the perfect place to indulge his new taste for Italian design. On a plateau of high ground, overlooking a spectacular sweep of Wiltshire countryside, he found the site for his house. In 1717 he bought Stourton Manor and the surrounding estate, pulled down the near-derelict manor house and planned the Palladian villa that would herald a new era of country living for the Hoares.

Opposite Henry Hoare 'the Good' holds the plans for his new house; painted by Michael Dahl about 1722

Below left The east front, depicted between construction of the Library and Picture Gallery wings in 1792 and the addition of the portico in 1838–9; watercolour by John Buckler

Below right The west, garden front today

The building of the house

The East front of Stourhead in Wiltshire the Seat of Henry Hoare Esq.

Henry seems to have been a cautious character, although he was given to radical thought at times. He called a meeting in 1716 to galvanise other philanthropists to 'consult upon the most effectual methods for relieving the Sick and Needy'. Henry waved a ten-pound note and urged action, which eventually resulted in the foundation of what was to become the Westminster Hospital and, eventually, other London hospitals offering free medical care to those who really needed it. But, in matters of business and personal expenditure, he was careful to err on the side of moderation and wait until money was to hand.

Above Colen Campbell's design for Stourhead was published in his *Vitruvius Britannicus* in 1725

When, partly as a result of the enormous profits (around £28,000) Hoare's Bank had made from the notorious South Sea Trading Company, he was able to start building his new villa on the acres he had named 'Stourhead' to reflect the source of the river that flowed through his land, his brother-in-law came to his aid. William Benson was an enthusiastic amateur architect, whose appointment to the post formerly held by Wren was a mystery to many. But William's deputy was the talented Colen Campbell, who had done much to promote the Palladian revival with a three-volume work, *Vitruvius Britannicus* or the *British Architect,* which was in effect a catalogue of design. Beautifully engraved plans, elevations and sections showing designs of classical purity and good taste, tempted men of substance, such as Henry. The book, published at the beginning of a boom in eighteenth-century country-house building, was influential and popular.

  Henry not only bought the first volume of the book but also employed its creator, the Scottish Campbell, to oversee the building of a suitably Palladian house on his hilltop site. He and Campbell worked with builder Nathaniel Ireson, whose team built the villa.

The foundations for the new house at Stourhead were laid in 1721, four years after Henry's purchase of the estate. By that time Colen Campbell's work had become well known and he was able to point to the palatial Wanstead House in Essex, which he had designed for Sir Richard Child, and the remodelling of the front of Burlington House (now the Royal Academy) in Piccadilly for Richard Boyle, the 3rd Earl of Burlington, who became a champion of the Scottish architect. Stourhead was finished in 1725, when its complete design was published in the third volume of Campbell's *Vitruvius Britannicus.*

Above The tomb of Henry Hoare 'the Good' in St Peter's church, which he repaired and renovated

Henry was careful in overseeing the work, planning how the house and estate should be run in the future and in buying household equipment and furniture for the house as construction proceeded.

  He was equally involved with the little parish church of St Peter which sits at the bottom of the hill, just a few minutes' walk from Stourhead House. Henry was a loyal Tory and a supporter of the Church of England. As the new patron of St Peter's, he undertook a complete refurbishment of the church, taking out the rood screen and anything else that smacked of the 'old religion'. A new altar, box pews and galleries were installed while splendid new church silver – a chalice and offertory plate and a silver-gilt flagon – were gifts to mark his new responsibilities.

and wide. He would notice it has been redecorated and would scratch his head over most of the characters hanging on the walls – the family descendants he never met.

Stourhead was one of the first grand Palladian-style villas to be built in England and, as such, it follows the correct tradition, where the carriage entrance leads to the *piano nobile*, or main floor, where are arranged the state rooms, each carefully sized to sit in perfect harmony with the others.

Underneath, in a semi-basement, lie the far less elegant but necessary 'engine rooms' of the house – the kitchens, sculleries and offices.

What Henry would not know is that the two rooms flanking this front were added by his great-grandson, Richard Colt Hoare, in 1792. One housed his library, the other his collection of paintings. He would have been shocked to have learnt that his wonderful house was gutted by fire in 1902, but was rebuilt almost as it was before. The Library and Picture Gallery were undamaged by the flames.

That Henry intended to make Stourhead a great part of his life is not in doubt. On 27 January 1725 his meticulously kept accounts showed that the total spent on the building up to that date was £10,150 10s 5d – which included £50 0s 9d for his gift of silver communion plate to St Peter's church. Three years earlier, Henry had made his will, decreeing that he should be buried 'in a leaden coffin' in the new family vault that he had built underneath the chancel at St Peter's, rather than at the family church of St Dunstan in the West, opposite Hoare's Bank in Fleet Street. He stipulated that the burial should take place in 'a private manner'. That burial, probably earlier than he had expected, followed his death in March 1725 at the age of 47, just as his new house was nearing completion.

If Henry were to visit his house today, he might be puzzled by its appearance; still starkly Palladian, but with an open portico rather than the pilasters (flat columns set against the wall) and massive triangular pediment with imposing steps that he decided on in 1721. He would also notice that this east-facing front has been greatly enlarged, with the addition of a pavilion on either side, virtually tripling the length of the building.

Today's entrance is much closer to Colen Campbell's original design, abandoned by Henry, when the villa was built.

It is pleasant to think that he would have heartily approved of the four massive stone basins flanking the portico; they are decorated with the perching eagles that are the Hoare family emblem. He would not have recognised the three lead statues atop the portico – they once stood in the Temple of Apollo in the garden and were moved to their new grand positions in the early twentieth century. Henry understood the rationale of Palladian building, where the dimensions of all spaces are related; he would recognise the Entrance Hall, built as a perfect cube, 30 feet tall, high

Opposite The open portico was originally proposed by Campbell, but was not implemented until 1838–9

Left The portico is flanked by stone basins, on which eagles perch

Below The statues on the roof of the house were moved from the Temple of Apollo (see p. 26)

Stourhead House was intended to be the main country home for Henry 'the Good' and his wife, Jane. However, when Henry died in 1725, Jane found herself moving to Stourhead alone with her young son Henry. They continued work on the estate, which included bringing a water supply to the house and eventually creating a garden.

At this stage Henry, who would inherit Stourhead on his mother's death, was a young man of nineteen and not interested in making gardens. That would come later, and, when it did, it was magnificent. He did, however, fulfil his obligation to complete the house, spending £10,000 on building and several thousand on furniture in the ten years after his father's death.

It is tempting to think that Jane and Henry I planned their country house together, furnishing rooms in the way that best suited them. Over the centuries, the shape, size and function of the rooms have changed, so it is not always easy to see how the couple arranged their living space. For example, the room that is now known as the Little Dining Room, opening off the Inner Hall, with windows facing south, started life as a garden room. Before the Library was added in 1792, this room had a door and a twin flight of steps leading down into the garden. Maybe Jane sat here in the morning, enjoying the sun before taking a stroll outside.

The Saloon, greatly enlarged by Jane's son, Henry, in 1744, is shown on Colen Campbell's plans as a chapel, but it has been used as a grand reception room and a dining room, as has the next-door Column Room. Although Henry did not begin his landscape garden below Stourhead House until a few years after his mother's death in 1741, Jane did have a garden to the south of the villa. Today's visitors may take a path beside a rhododendron 'hedge' to the south lawn where a walled garden was planted soon after the house was finished. This was replaced sometime in the following sixty years by a large lawned area softened by many trees including variegated sycamores and tulip trees.

Before Jane died, her son Henry made his first addition to the garden, a Fir Walk on the hillside south-west of the house. A contemporary description, which dates this Walk at around 1733, tells us it was of 'considerable extent, of the softest mossy turf, bordered on each side by stately Scotch Firs'.

Later c.1746–7 an obelisk was built of Chilmark stone surmounted by a solar disc, forming a full stop to the length of the Walk.

Opposite The Little Dining Room started out as a garden room

Below The Hoare eagle emblem was used elsewhere on the estate, as here at the entrance to the Spread Eagle Inn

The Hoare family emblem of a silver double-headed eagle on a black background within an engrailed (serrated) silver border was first used officially when Henry 'the Magnificent' was granted arms in 1776. But it seems the family used this device unofficially for many years before this. The idea for the emblem may have come from the old name of their early Fleet Street premises, which was known as the Black Spread Eagle.

Henry 'the Magnificent'

Left Henry Hoare 'the Magnificent'; painted by Michael Dahl

Henry, who in later life took his responsibilities seriously, managed to enjoy a short spell of misspent youth during holidays at another Hoare family home at Quarley, near Andover in Hampshire. He confessed to his grandson and heir, Richard Colt Hoare, that there had been a time when he enjoyed hunting, shooting and drinking with his friends. But Henry was a Hoare, devoted to the family business, and he quickly developed more sober habits, when he realised that this 'gay and dissolute style of life' was affecting his health.

He was fortunate in many ways: Stourhead, a prosperous country estate, was his after his mother's death and he inherited the bank premises and a large share of the business, as well as other freehold property in London. Throughout his life he was entitled to half the bank profits, which made him considerably wealthy. It was the way he used this wealth that

Henry 'the Magnificent' was not so fortunate in his family life. He was 21 when he married Anne, the daughter of Lord and Lady Masham. Anne, just eighteen, died a few days after the birth of their baby daughter, Ann, within a year of marriage. This child died when she was eight and is buried at Stourton. He and his second wife, Susanna Colt, whom he married in 1728, the year following Anne's death, had three children, a son, Henry, and two daughters, Susanna (Sukey) and Anne (Nanny). This Anne was born the year following the death of her little half-sister. His wife, Susanna, died in 1743, when young Henry was thirteen and the girls eleven and six. Their father took care to secure their futures, but each died before he did, which caused him immense grief.

brought him the sobriquet 'Magnificent', spending splendidly, as he did, on a well-chosen collection of paintings and sculpture and, when the spirit moved him, devising a classical landscape at Stourhead that had no equal.

But Henry was no spendthrift. He attended assiduously to business at the bank, and he read widely, becoming familiar with poets and writers such as Milton, Pope, Virgil and Ovid, whose moral stories of heroic figures journeying bravely through classical landscapes surely had an influence on the garden he eventually designed.

Another influence was his uncle, William Benson, the fervent admirer of all things Palladian. Benson's own small classical villa,

Above left The Hon. Anne Masham, the first wife of Henry 'the Magnificent'; painted by Michael Dahl about 1725

Above right Carlo Maratta's *Marchese Niccolo Maria Pallavacini guided to the Temple of Virtue by Apollo* was one of the Italian Old Masters acquired by Henry Hoare 'the Magnificent'.

Wilbury, at Newton Toney near Salisbury, became Henry's in 1734, and it was probably here, through his uncle, that he met the architect Henry Flitcroft, the sculptor Michael Rysbrack and the painter John Wootton, each of whom had enormous input at Stourhead, in the garden and the house.

Henry waited until he was in his early thirties to travel abroad, to see the landscapes he so admired in art and literature. He had started to collect paintings before his belated Grand Tour, which started in 1738, and continued to visit the sale rooms in Paris and Rome, shipping the seventeenth- and eighteenth-century masters back to Stourhead.

Classical inspiration

Above The benches in the Pantheon are decorated with classical scenes to match the classical inspiration of Henry's garden

Opposite The Temple of Flora

Henry had been master of Stourhead for several years before his plans for a landscape garden below the house took shape. He must have spent much time standing on the high ground gazing down at the few trees, the two ponds, the river, planning the shape of his garden and waiting for the inspiration that would guide its creation.

He read classical literature and studied paintings. He grieved for his first wife and young daughter and loved his three children by his second wife, Susanna. He took himself off to Italy where the treasures of the past literally littered the squares and the streets, and where the evidence of what he saw as nobler times fired his imagination. Most historians agree that Henry's final inspiration for the garden at Stourhead came from one of his well-thumbed books, Virgil's *Aeneid*, the story of heroic Aeneas, whose long adventure-filled journey from his home in war-torn Troy, to found a Roman culture, struck several chords.

The virtues of devotion to duty and reverence for the gods, shown by Aeneas through all his trials on the long journey, would have resonated with Henry – even though those gods were ones far removed from his own, thoroughly Protestant, maker. He too was founding a dynasty based on a place and he wanted

Below Henry Hoare 'the Magnificent'; painted by Samuel Woodforde c.1795–1800 after William Hoare

to create something whose meaning and beauty would last through the generations.

By 1744, a year after his wife, Susanna, died, Henry was ready to begin the work that was to occupy him for much of the rest of his life.

By this time he had decided that the allegorical journey through his landscape garden would take place around a lake, which he would create by merging the existing ponds and by building a dam to raise the water level. He would plant groups of trees on the slopes around the lakeside and these would be interspersed with buildings and other features, each giving meaning to the winding walk along the banks of the water.

On a hillside, overlooking a spring called Paradise Well, not far inside today's garden entrance stands the Temple of Flora, Henry's first building. When he and architect Henry Flitcroft planned this one-roomed building with its Tuscan Doric columns, overlooking a stream that was to become a lake, it was named the Temple of Ceres (after the Roman goddess of fertility and farming).

A new master for Stourhead

Above Coplestone Warre Bampfylde's view of the garden c.1775, showing the Palladian Bridge, the Temple of Apollo and the Pantheon. The planting is still quite immature

Henry was still writing enthusiastically to his daughter, Sukey, and her children about the changes he was making at Stourhead in 1776, when he was in his early seventies. He wrote of the new Grotto entrance being finished in time for her visit and, later, when she and the children were staying with him, wrote to his son-in-law: 'Thank God they are all fine and well, and now make nothing of walking round the gardens; and I mounted the Tower Thursday with the dear children.'

His concern for his immediate family's health was understandable. His younger daughter, Anne (Nanny), who married her cousin Richard, Henry's nephew, had died in 1759, a few months after giving birth to Colt Hoare. The boy's father, a partner in the bank, soon remarried and Colt Hoare was brought up with his half-brothers and sisters at the family villa, Barn Elms, at Mortlake. He spent his holidays at Stourhead with his grandfather, who he described as: 'Tall and comely in person, elegant in his manners and address and well versed in polite literature.'

Colt Hoare, then a child of six, saw the round Temple of Apollo being built in 1765, high on a hillside at the western side of the lake. The design by Flitcroft was based on a Roman building at Baalbek in Lebanon as shown in Robert Wood's *Ruins of Balbec,* a book owned by Henry Hoare. The boy would have seen his grandfather's enthusiasm for his next project, a tower which was to be built in honour, not of Roman gods and goddesses,

Henry's solution was surprising and caused resentment in the family. His nephew and one-time son-in-law, Richard of Barn Elms, should inherit the freehold of the bank. Richard's son, Richard Colt Hoare, would become owner of his grandfather's beloved Stourhead, on the condition that he severed all ties with the bank, where he was working at the time.

Henry handed Stourhead over to Colt Hoare in 1783 and retired to his new house at Clapham where he died in 1785 at the age of eighty.

Above View from the Chinese Umbrella, F.M. Piper, 1779

Right King Alfred's Tower was Henry Flitcroft's last work for Henry Hoare II

but Alfred the Great, King of Wessex from 871 to 899 and successful defender of his people against the marauding Vikings. It was to be a copy of St Mark's Campanile in Venice – until Henry saw the imposing Gothic tower built by his friend Charles Hamilton at Painshill. Stourhead's tower would be in similar style – but three times taller. The triangular tower, with its viewing platform, designed by Flitcroft, was completed by 1772 and situated on Kingsettle Hill, two miles north-west of Stourhead, where King Alfred is said to have raised his standard before trouncing the invading Vikings.

Other garden buildings and ornaments – a Chinese 'umbrella' on the southern slopes, a 'Gothick greenhouse', a 'Druid's Cell' and various river gods, have since disappeared.

Henry was not easy in his mind during the final years. The huge national debt, brought about by war, could make the bank vulnerable. His own personal losses (his last daughter, Sukey, died in 1783) were increasingly hard to bear. He was determined at least to secure the future of Stourhead, the place he most loved. It was imperative that the estate must be divorced entirely from the Bank, even if that weakened the business.

Colt Hoare's move to Stourhead in 1783 did not begin well. Although he married that year and was very happy with his bride, the vivacious and intelligent Hester Lyttelton, there was still resentment in the family over the arrangements put in place by his grandfather.

Colt Hoare himself felt that he had had no choice in being torn away from the bank where he was settled as an Agent (a family probationer) with assured future prospects, while his father, who had expected to inherit Stourhead, lived with the humiliation of seeing his son there in his stead. Henry's decisions had, in effect, split the family into two self-supporting branches – the London bankers and the landed gentry at Stourhead.

Tension gave way to tragedy, as Colt Hoare's young wife died in 1785, after giving birth to their second child, who did not survive. Within weeks of Hester's demise, his grandfather, Henry 'the Magnificent', was also dead. Colt Hoare, unable to settle with his grief, ordered so many mourning clothes that Hester's funeral had to be delayed for a week to allow time for their manufacture. Very soon he fled England for the Continent where, apart from a brief visit home in 1787, the year of his father's death, he stayed for four years, leaving Stourhead in the care of a steward. His only child, a son, Henry Richard, born in 1784, was also left to the care of others.

The distraction of travel eased Colt Hoare's mind. He had continued his classical education while serving with the bank, and on reaching Rome early in 1786 he wrote home to say that he was happily employed drawing the antiquities he saw everywhere: 'There is so much work for my pencil that I know not when I shall be able to get away.' He made friends and was entertained with soirées, concerts, dining parties and even to a meeting with the Jacobite 'Young Pretender', Charles Edward Stuart, and his daughter, the Duchess of Albany.

It was a long time before he could be tempted home to Stourhead and the prospect of a life so different, but when, in 1801, the French Revolutionary Wars threatened insecurity abroad, he returned. He brought with him portfolios of his own drawings, many paintings to add to his grandfather's collection and a deeper understanding and appreciation of the past, that was to further his career as a historian and his position as owner of one of England's great estates.

Opposite Richard Colt Hoare and his son Henry; painted by Samuel Woodforde c.1795–6

Below The tomb of Richard Colt Hoare's wife, Hester, who died young in 1785

Samuel Woodforde's large painting of Colt Hoare gazing wistfully into the middle distance of a classical landscape with his young son, Henry Richard, trying to attract his attention, shows a man bent on pursuit of scholarship. Woodforde said that he found his subject 'a shy man to strangers, but liberal and steady in his attachments'. Original letters on display at Stourhead show that the relationship between Colt Hoare and his son was a difficult one. As Henry grew up, he spent time as an in-patient being treated for nervous disorders, although he became an excellent first-class cricketer and a member of the Middlesex Cricket Club, for which he played between 1823 and 1824. He died, before his father, in 1836.

A scholar's approach

When Richard Colt Hoare returned to Stourhead in July 1791, he was a wealthy man, ennobled by the death, in 1787, of his father who had been elevated to the baronetcy a couple of years earlier.

Sir Richard Colt Hoare, now 2nd Baronet, owned 11,000 acres, which brought in the massive sum of £10,000 a year, and he was in a position to turn his full attention to the home he had largely ignored for six years.

Above Exterior of Colt Hoare's Library

Colt Hoare venerated the Old Masters, as had his grandfather, but unlike Henry 'the Magnificent', he also became a champion of contemporary British artists, including J.M.W. Turner, whom he commissioned to paint a series of watercolours of Salisbury. Turner also copied Colt Hoare's own drawing of Lake Avernus, turning it into *Lake Avernus with Aeneas and the Cumean Sibyl*. John Constable visited Stourhead in 1811, drawing a view of the gardens which now hangs at the Fogg Art Museum, Cambridge, Massachusetts. Samuel Woodforde, Francis Nicholson and Henry Thomson were three other painters he admired and whose work he commissioned.

Colt Hoare also employed furniture-maker and carver Thomas Chippendale the Younger, who lived and worked at Stourhead for several years, making exquisite furniture for the two new wings. The support of men such as Colt Hoare saved Chippendale from bankruptcy in 1804.

The Picture Gallery sits above the basement, where Colt Hoare kept his archaeological museum.

Left Colt Hoare's fine antiquarian library included John Carter's *Specimens of the Ancient Sculpture and Painting Now Remaining in this Kingdom*, 1780–7

Right Egyptian revival decoration on the Library desk

Presumably the great sorrow he had endured grew less with the years, but there is no doubt that the travels, engendered by his grief, had broadened his knowledge and interests to such an extent that he was able to fulfil his scholarly ambitions.

He decided that Stourhead was not large enough for his books and paintings so, very soon after his return, he designed the two large wings to the north and south of the house, thus greatly altering its appearance. These pavilions became a picture gallery and a superb library, where Colt Hoare catalogued and displayed his enormous collection of historical and topographical books. These are there no longer, but volumes collected from other Hoare family homes fill the shelves, along with Colt Hoare's own manuscripts and the journals he kept of his travels.

The Library and the Picture Gallery are outstanding examples of Regency taste.

A new perspective

Henry's landscape garden had been well-tended during Colt Hoare's six-year absence, but no changes had been made. Stourhead's new owner looked at the scene with a fresh eye and with an extensive knowledge of the trees and shrubs now available to gardeners.

When his Library and Picture Gallery wings were complete, the front of the house looked completely different, so a new driveway – the one in use today – was made. Colt Hoare moved the gatehouse – all that remained of the ancient buildings – to its present position, marking the main entrance to his house.

He made known his dislike of 'nature overcrowded with buildings' – especially if those buildings were at odds with each other, removing some of his grandfather's objects that were neither Palladian nor Gothic in style. The Chinese Umbrella and painted Turkish Tent had already disappeared, but a Venetian Seat on the terrace near the house was removed, while a replica Coade Stone Borghese Vase and two busts were taken to the Temple of Flora.

The 'greenhouse of false Gothic', a 'Chinese Alcove' and the (by now unsafe) wooden bridge over the north of the lake were removed, the latter replaced by a ferry.

Henry Hoare's 'Hermitage', built on the way to the Temple of Apollo, was removed later (Henry had written in 1771 to alert granddaughter Harriot about its construction, adding 'I believe I shall put myself in to be the hermit'). Colt Hoare added the rock-work boathouse near the Temple of Flora, to house the ferry that replaced the wooden bridge and he 'Gothicised' the cottage between the Grotto and the Pantheon with the addition of a rustic porch and seat.

Turning his attention to the village, he removed cottages that hid the church from view, and added Gothic touches to the remaining buildings that matched the church parapet. The ever-busy Stourton Inn saw a name change, as the sign showing the River Stour was removed and that depicting Colt Hoare's family crest, the Spread Eagle, prominently displayed.

Opposite Colt Hoare extended the entrance front by adding pavilions at both ends

Below *Prospect of Stonehenge from the South-West* from the library of Colt Hoare who was an expert on the antiquities of Wiltshire

Colt Hoare's own studious and observant nature and interest in the past, which had been stimulated by his travels abroad, remained with him for the rest of his life. He enlisted the help of other amateur archaeologists, such as William Cunnington and his close friend Richard Fenton, to explore the topography and history of Wiltshire and Wales. He and Cunnington made the first recorded excavation at Stonehenge and went on to examine and record 379 burial sites on Salisbury Plain. Colt Hoare's *Ancient Histories of North and South Wiltshire* (1812–19) are scholarly works, still well-regarded. Drawings by Colt Hoare were also engraved for his friend William Coxe's *Historical Tour in Monmouthshire*.

Prospect of STONEHENGE from the Southwest.

Planting on a grand scale

It had always been Henry Hoare's intention that the approach to the gardens should be from the house, allowing the drama of that sudden first view of the lake and the church below. Colt Hoare built gravel paths to make the walk easier, but with an entrance from the village. This, with a new path from the stone bridge to the rock arch on the north side of the lake, by-passing the climb to the Temple of Apollo, meant that visitors strolled around on one level in an anti-clockwise direction, losing some of the dramatic impact. The 50 gardeners found they had a new daily task – sweeping the gravel to keep it clean and level. The paths extended around the north-eastern end of the lake between Diana's Basin and the Lily Pond to enlarge the garden, bringing part of the park outside into the pleasure grounds.

A French painter, whose work was beloved by both Colt Hoare and his grandfather, Henry 'the Magnificent', received an unusual tribute in 1820 when Colt Hoare created the lake below the dam. This fourteen-acre sheet of water was named 'Gaspar' in tribute to Gaspar Dughet, whose scenes of rural Roman beauty inspired much of the Stourhead landscape. Dughet, who had died in 1675, was Nicolas Poussin's brother-in-law and pupil.

From 1791 onwards Colt Hoare began to plant extensively, clothing the southern banks with many more trees, including acers, horse chestnut, birch, catalpa, hawthorn, ash, holly, tulip trees, liquidambar, plane trees, cherry, oak, robinia, lime and swamp cypress. He also underplanted with laurel and rhododendron, creating a sea of green beneath the trees.

In 1815 he placed a memorial tablet, dedicated to the memory of his grandfather, Henry, at the base of the Obelisk at the end of Fir Walk. Colt Hoare's interests extended to natural history in general. He was a member of the newly formed Linnean Society (inaugurated in 1788) which continues to document the flora and fauna of the world. Colt Hoare's special interest was in the collection of the tender

pelargoniums, plants native to South and eastern Africa, Madagascar, New Zealand and Australia. He bred new hybrids, increasing his original collection of 53 varieties to more than 600 by 1821. Then the collection was housed in a large conservatory near the Library on the south-west corner of the house. Today a greenhouse in the Walled Garden contains more than sixty varieties of these beautiful plants, and there are pelargoniums in the Hoarea section of geraniums named after Richard Colt Hoare.

Above and left The Victoran greenhouse in the Walled Garden today houses a collection of rare pelargoniums inspired by that created by Colt Hoare

Opposite The Pantheon with the autumn colours of *Liriodendron tulipfera*

Colt Hoare did not remarry. He never revisited Europe after his return home in 1791 but he spent much time away from Stourhead, studying the archaeology and history of different areas of the British Isles. He was elected a Fellow of the Royal Society in 1792 and was made a Fellow of the Society of Antiquaries of London. But by the time he reached his early sixties, deaf and often crippled with gout and rheumatism, he did not move far from Stourhead where he found solace for his ill health in his library, picture gallery, museum and garden. He died, aged eighty, in 1838 and is buried in St Peter's church. There is a memorial monument to him in Salisbury Cathedral.

Henry Hugh and Hugh Richard Hoare
Victorian guardians

Sir Richard Colt Hoare died, after becoming increasingly housebound, in May 1838. His only son, Henry, had died two years before, so Stourhead went to his half-brother and good friend, Henry Hugh Hoare, a partner in the bank and, like Colt Hoare, a Fellow of the Society of Antiquaries. Henry Hugh, who became the 3rd Baronet, already had a country house – Wavendon, in Buckinghamshire – but he did not neglect Stourhead.

It was he who fulfilled architect Colen Campbell's original design for the grand entrance, building the massive open portico as you see it today, to replace the pediment with its steeply rising flights of steps chosen by his forebear, Henry 'the Good'. In 1839–40 he rebuilt the Obelisk that had marked the end of Henry 'the Magnificent's' Fir Walk; it was crumbling dangerously, so was remade in Bath stone. Fifteen years later it had to be repaired again after being struck by lightning.

Henry Hugh, not much younger than Colt Hoare, lived only three years after inheriting the estate, which, in 1841, passed to his son, Hugh Richard, also a partner in the bank.

Hugh Richard did what Henry 'the Magnificent' would have wanted – retired from the bank (thus severing the connection that had been made again when his father inherited) and, with his wife, Anne Tyrwhitt-Drake, moved to Stourhead in 1845 to live the life of a country gentleman and devote himself to the improvement of his 11,000-acre estate.

Opposite **Sir Henry Hugh Hoare, 3rd Bt (1762–1841);** painted by Prince Hoare, son of William Hoare of Bath, c.1780

Below **Sir Hugh Richard Hoare, 4th Bt (1787–1857);** painted by an unknown British artist

His annual allowance from Hoare's of £5,200, soon rising to £8,000, allowed him to improve the farms and their buildings. The large letters 'H.R.H.' visible on cottages and farm buildings across the estate were not a reference to royalty, but to Hugh Richard, who built new stables, barns, lambing and cattle sheds, wagon-houses, farmhouses and cottages. He put snug tiled roofs on previously thatched cottages and saw to it that land drains were built and maintained, new fields were hedged and fenced and cultivated and that hedges were cut back at the proper time. Hugh Richard separated the park from Stourhead House with a good iron fence that stands today. The population of Stourton had risen to more than 650, so Hugh Richard, patron of St Peter's, did the right thing and built a new south aisle to accommodate would-be church-goers.

He planted spruce, larch and Scots pine commercially and kept up to date with new species of trees brought into the country at that time by plant hunters such as David Douglas and William Lobb. Douglas fir, hemlock and spruce, the 'Monkey Puzzle' tree (*Araucaria araucana*), the giant western red cedar (*Thuja plicata*), the enormous coast redwood (*Sequoia sempervirens*) in the gardens, date from this time and are among the earliest trees of this type in Britain.

Records of improvements and planting were kept in the 'Stourhead Annals', instigated by Colt Hoare and kept until 1860, when they were discontinued until 1894.

Stourhead passed in direct line from father to son only twice. Henry 'the Magnificent' inherited from his father 'the Good' while Hugh Richard was the other son to inherit. He was 54 and married, but had no children, so when he died in 1857 ten years after his wife, Anne, the estate passed to his nephew Henry Ainslie Hoare.

Henry Ainslie and Augusta

During Ainslie's time at the bank, an anecdote told how, one day, he asked a clerk to have documents ready for signature as early as possible. This done, he mounted a horse waiting for him at London Bridge, rode to Epsom where he watched, and presumably betted on, the Derby, before cantering back to London in time to lock up at 5pm.

Left Augusta, Lady Hoare (d.1903); painted by Lord Leighton in 1858

In the Entrance Hall are two striking portraits that tell, perhaps more than any others, of the lives and characters of the sitters.

The sombre and sorrowful gaze of Augusta Frances Clayton East, arms wrapped protectively around her elegant black-clad figure, speaks of wistful regret. The tips of her long fingers are hidden by the fine mourning material; her glossy black hair, emphasising the pale beauty of her fine-featured face, is enhanced by a dark red rose. Behind her are a cloudy deep blue sky, an orange tree and a classical sculpture.

Augusta's husband, the racy Sir Henry Ainslie Hoare, 5th Baronet, who inherited Stourhead in 1857, hangs on the opposite side of the room, gazing sardonically out of the frame, wavy hair brushed back and parted in the middle, small moustache and half-beard hiding his mouth. You feel his hand, thrust into the pocket of his jacket, is clenched. Augusta loved Stourhead and her family. Henry loved hunting and horseracing, the thrill of politics and the lure of France. Above all, he loved to gamble. It is doubtful that they loved each other, but it is said that Henry Ainslie, domiciled mainly in France, always came home to their London residence or to Stourhead when he was ill with gout, so that Augusta could nurse him.

They started their life together happily enough, honeymooning at Stourhead in 1845. Augusta spent her early married life caring for her mother and then for her two children, Gussy, a daughter born in the first year of her marriage and Charles, who arrived the following year. Her husband became a 'confidential clerk' at the family bank in 1847, but he was dismissed (with an allowance) within a year. He moved to Paris, followed a few months later by Augusta and their children. When some of the partners made noises about inviting him back into the business, they were discouraged by an influential customer, the Duke of Hamilton, who told them of his reckless gambling. In the early 1850s he sold his interest in the family business to pay off debts.

France was their home until Ainslie inherited Stourhead in January 1857. Two and a half years earlier, their only son, Charles, aged eight, had died, leaving the family estate once again without a direct heir. He was buried at Sablonville in France.

Ainslie, Augusta and daughter Gussy, then eleven years old, arrived at Stourhead in June, staying until late October, when they returned to France, establishing a pattern that would persist, certainly for Augusta and occasionally for Ainslie, for the next three decades.

Below The Hoare's daughter, 'Gussy', who often brought her children to stay at Stourhead; painted by Lord Leighton in 1860

Absentee owners

Neither Henry Ainslie nor Augusta settled on Stourhead as their permanent family home, although it is clear from her diaries that the happiest times of her often melancholy life were spent here.

She established a routine of spending the whole of the summer and most of the autumn at Stourhead, first with her daughter, Gussy, and then with Gussy's four children, who came to stay with her when they grew old enough. She would spend the winter at their London home in Eaton Place, or in France. She and her husband led virtually separate social lives, he basing himself mainly in London and Paris. The portrait of Augusta in the Entrance Hall was painted by her lifelong friend, Frederic, Lord Leighton, in Paris in 1858, the year after she became mistress of Stourhead. He began it in January, at the beginning of the year, soon after one of the last entries in her diary for 1857 which read, plaintively: 'Another year full of pain and a little pleasure'. It is interesting to speculate whether the 'little pleasure' might have been that found at her new home.

When Ainslie first inherited, he showed interest in his house to the extent of building a new fountain on the lawn, so that Augusta could see it from her room. She later turned this lawn into a graveyard for her dogs. He also oversaw the replacement of the old oak bridge near the Pantheon with the iron structure which is still in place but it seems this is the extent of the building programme during his 37 years' ownership of Stourhead.

Sir Henry Ainslie Hoare obviously appreciated the good husbandry of his predecessor, Hugh Richard, paying tribute to his uncle with a stained-glass window, dedicated to his memory, in St Peter's church. The window was one of several commissioned by Ainslie, following the fashionable reintroduction of brightly coloured glass.

Opposite The garden buildings fell into disrepair during Ainslie's time. The Temple of Apollo by a *Country Life* photographer before restoration

Below Ainslie's Iron Bridge today

He left the day-to-day management of the estate, the farms and the commercial woodland in the capable hands of his steward, Robert Shackleton, who kept 'daybooks' as records of what was done, showing regular correspondence with Ainslie and meetings with him when he visited Stourhead. A little planting was done in the garden, including the introduction of blue cedar, cypress trees, spruce and pine.

While Augusta later referred to Stourhead in her diaries as her 'beloved home', Sir Henry saw it as the place he brought friends to in the autumn for hunting, shooting and fishing and enjoying a brief social whirl in the country. When he was entertaining in London he would send to Wiltshire for basket loads of fresh produce for his parties at Eaton Place.

Under shutters

'How little I thought I was leaving my beloved home for ever,' wrote Augusta in her journal when she left Stourhead a few days after her husband in late 1885.

It is ironic that Stourhead, built as a family home, was rarely inhabited by children. Richard Colt Hoare's lonely son spent his childhood here, while Henry 'the Magnificent's' son and daughters lived at Stourhead for part of the year. Henry 'the Magnificent' enjoyed entertaining the 'dear children' (his grandchildren) here. But it was not until Stourhead became the summer home for Augusta's four grandchildren that the house and garden became alive with the shouts and laughter of young people.
The happiest times of Augusta's life seem to have been, according to her journals, those spent at Stourhead with the young Marcia, Julius, Leila and Zoe Angerstein. They would ride in the woods and gardens in donkey-chairs and wagonettes, or make expeditions to the Convent or Alfred's Tower with well-filled picnic hampers. There were parties in the Picture Gallery when children from the village were invited to the 'big house' to enjoy tea and games.

Right Ainslie and Augusta loved to picnic at the Convent in the woods, now a private residence

These happy times came abruptly to an end in 1885, when the house was shut up. There were intimations all was not well in 1883, as valuable paintings and books were sold (see below), but when Ainslie failed to win the East Somerset seat for the Tories in the General Election, he decided to move away entirely.

Ainslie, who had been educated at Eton and Cambridge, was not without some social conscience. He served in Parliament as the Liberal member for New Windsor from 1865–6 and for Chelsea from 1868–74. But when Gladstone's Liberals won the General Election of 1880, he became disillusioned with their policies. Moreover, as a landowner, albeit managing the Stourhead estate through his steward Robert Shackleton, he witnessed at first hand the slump in agriculture.

Above The Stourhead garden in the late nineteenth century

He defected to the Tories in the mid-seventies and was swift to sign up for the Primrose League, formed a couple of years after Disraeli's death in 1881. The League (named after Disraeli's favourite flower), which soon attracted a quarter of a million members (Henry Ainslie was member number 65), became one of the leading political organisations of the day, and Ainslie one of its most popular speakers, opposing 'one man, one vote' and supporting imperialism. *Vanity Fair* magazine made him the subject of one of its famous 'Spy' cartoons. But, although he stood as Tory candidate for East Somerset in 1885, he lost, and it was at this point he decided he could no longer afford to keep Stourhead open.

Failing to find a tenant, he closed the house and spent much of the rest of his life in France. Taken ill at Nice in March 1894, he returned to England where he died at his London house in Eaton Place. He was buried at Stourhead.

Hard times force sales

Great estates were hit by hard times during the agricultural depression of the late nineteenth century. Stourhead, no exception, was then owned by the largely absentee 5th Baronet, Sir Henry Ainslie Hoare, who was forced to sell some of the treasures bought and commissioned by Henry 'the Magnificent' and Sir Richard Colt Hoare. The first heirloom sale was held in 1883, and a series of paintings of Salisbury by J.M.W. Turner, his *Lake Avernus*, Poussin's *Rape of the Sabines*, Francis Nicholson's watercolours of the garden and Colt Hoare's unequalled library of topographical books, all left Stourhead. Almost twenty years later, in 1902, the central part of the house was gutted by fire but, miraculously, most of the ground-floor contents were rescued, while the Library and Picture Gallery escaped unscathed.

A revival and a fire

By the time the 6th Baronet, Sir Henry Hugh Arthur Hoare, and his wife, Alda, had their portraits painted by the romantic and sentimental Irish artist St George Hare, they were well on the way to saving Stourhead. It is thanks to this remarkable couple, who, in their different ways, made devotion to their country estate their life's work, that Stourhead is open to visitors today. It is they who furthered the work in the house, garden and estate, preserving what would relate the story of the Hoares who had gone before.

And it was this Sir Henry who, when the time came, teased out a way to ensure that Stourhead would not be divided or demolished because of heavy death duties.

Sir Henry was not involved in the family business, but he was a director of Lloyds Bank. At the time a fire was discovered, on 16 April 1902, he was in Salisbury, attending a meeting at Lloyds. He hastily chartered a train to Gillingham, where his pony and trap waited. He galloped all the way to Stourhead, where he joined the huge team of more than one hundred people who had gathered to help rescue the first-floor furniture, paintings, silver and ornaments. He was interviewed by a reporter from the *Bristol Mercury*, who reported: 'He seemed to take the matter somewhat coolly, if outward appearances count for anything, and he walked up and down the lawn smoking cigarettes. But conversation with him revealed intense sorrow at what was taking place around him.'

Above The central block of the north front after the 1902 fire

Left Servants on the lawn after the fire

Their portraits flank that of Henry 'the Magnificent' in the Entrance Hall. Sir Henry, wearing white tie and a cutaway red jacket, sits in one of the Chippendale armchairs made for Colt Hoare in 1812. A cigarette trickling smoke, loosely held in his left hand, his arm resting on that of the chair, says that he is relaxed, but his direct gaze and his right hand, curled around the carved wood, shows a man ready for action. The observant will notice that the smoke forms the image of the face of his wife, Alda. She is portrayed with her dark hair piled high and wide to emphasise her strong features, a thick gold band around her neck, and also appears ready to spring from her chair. Her expression could be interpreted as triumphant.

And who could blame her? Her favourite painter created these portraits in 1907, the year that she and Sir Henry had seen the restoration of Stourhead completed, after the disastrous fire had gutted the central portion of the house.

Neither Sir Henry nor Alda was in any doubt what should happen following the fire: the house, which was fully insured, should be restored almost exactly as it had been. The couple, who had already lived in what they called 'the Cottage' (now the National Trust estate office) when they first moved to Stourhead, squared their shoulders and moved back for another two years, overseeing the restoration under Doran Webb and then Sir Aston Webb (no relation).

Above left Sir Henry Hoare 6th Bt (1865–1947); painted by St George Hare c.1909. He restored Stourhead after the fire in 1902 and gave the house, garden and estate to the National Trust in 1946

Above right Alda, Lady Hoare (d.1947); painted by St George Hare in 1909

A family home again

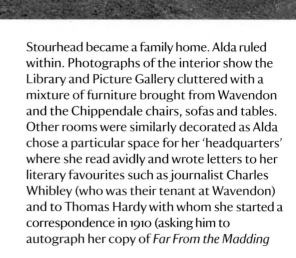

Henry and Alda devoted themselves to Stourhead for 53 years. They weathered the first years when they and their young son, Henry Colt Arthur, moved into 'the Cottage' in 1894 for almost three years, until the house, which had been shut up for nine years, was put in order. Sir Henry, who had lived at Wavendon in Buckinghamshire with his widowed mother and, after their marriage in 1887, with Alda, had managed the woodland at Stourhead since 1891. He began to clear the neglected gardens of overgrowth, repaired the Bristol Cross and the roof of the Grotto. During this time he began planting new ornamental trees and shrubs.

Stourhead became a family home. Alda ruled within. Photographs of the interior show the Library and Picture Gallery cluttered with a mixture of furniture brought from Wavendon and the Chippendale chairs, sofas and tables. Other rooms were similarly decorated as Alda chose a particular space for her 'headquarters' where she read avidly and wrote letters to her literary favourites such as journalist Charles Whibley (who was their tenant at Wavendon) and to Thomas Hardy with whom she started a correspondence in 1910 (asking him to autograph her copy of *Far From the Madding*

Crowd) that lasted for 25 years. Letters and postcards from him were found tucked in first editions of his novels in the Stourhead Library. Alda declared she was not a woman's woman and she terrorised her servants, dismissing them often for 'misbehaviour'. Yet she maintained a correspondence with both of Hardy's wives, first Emma and, after her death, Florence. Hardy wrote to Alda on Emma's death in 1912: 'As you know she was very fond of you, and I regret now that I did not bring her to see you at Stour Head. But, alas, I thought her in the soundest health and that there was plenty of time.'

Their only child, Henry Colt, graduated from Trinity College, Cambridge in 1910. A portrait of Harry, as his mother called him, hangs in the Saloon, casually dressed, tie tucked between the buttons of his shirt. It was painted by St George Hare in 1909 to celebrate the young man's 21st birthday. Harry graduated the following year and became his father's agent for all the estates, selling Oxenham in 1911.

Sir Henry and Alda did not falter when their home was destroyed by fire. The terrible blow when Harry was fatally wounded in Palestine in 1917 was almost too much for his grief-stricken parents. He had enlisted in the Dorset Yeomanry, fighting at Gallipoli in 1915. He was invalided out with double pneumonia and paratyphoid, before rejoining his regiment in Palestine, only to be shot in the attack on Mughar Ridge.

Opposite above Sir Henry and Lady Hoare with their son, Henry and dog 'Sweep'

Opposite below Lady Hoare's copy of *The Mayor of Casterbridge* by Thomas Hardy. She was a good friend of Hardy's two wives

The last son of Stourhead

A grieving Sir Henry recorded in the 'Stourhead Annals': 'During the attack on the Mughar Ridge [El Mughar, Palestine] he fell shot through the lungs on Nov 13th 1917. He remained on the field all night and was then removed 24 hours, by motor lorry ambulance to a dressing station, & after two or three days there to Raseltin Hospital, Alexandria where with varying ups & downs he struggled for life with the utmost patience, cheerfulness & pluck. His doctor, the matron & sister have all written to testify to this, & their regret at his loss. At two o'clock on Dec 19th died from Haemorrhage & heart failure. Capt Henry Colt Arthur Hoare at Raseltin Hospital, Alexandria (Egypt) and rest in the Hadra Military Cemetery there. Our only & the best of sons. He never grieved us by thought word or deed. He loved Stourhead, worked for it, & with us, all his life. He was deeply respected by all here who mourn his loss.'

Right Harry Hoare painted in 1914 in the uniform of the 1st Queen's Own Yeomanry by St George Hare. Harry's death in action in 1917 was a blow from which his parents never recovered

Securing Stourhead's future

Left The library at Wavendon, the Hoare's former home in Buckinghamshire

Weeks before Harry died Sir Henry and Alda had decided to accept an offer for their 'old' home, Wavendon in Buckinghamshire. Harry had telegraphed from the trenches to agree to the sale. Now they prevaricated, not knowing what to do for the best. But eventually, with advice from Harry's close friends and their solicitor, they decided to throw all their time and energy into Stourhead, casting off Wavendon. Stourhead had been Harry's childhood home and playground and he had, latterly, managed the estates; his presence was everywhere. They resolved that Stourhead must somehow survive without alteration.

Sir Henry, aware that heavily increased death duties could whittle the estate away to nothing, toyed with the idea of leaving the property to the National Trust. In 1925 he paid a salutary visit to Bryanston House in Dorset where the Portman family, unable to keep their Norman Shaw house and estate because of death duties, had put the family home and its contents on the market. Sir Henry vowed this would not happen at Stourhead. He wrote to Arthur Hervey Hoare, a partner in the bank: 'In [the sale] are included family portraits, photos of the family and most of the late man's intimate personal effects. It brought home to me what may happen when we are gone.'

Above James Lees-Milne, the National Trust's Historic Buildings Secretary from 1936 to 1951 and its Architectural Advisor from 1951 to 1976

Right The chimneypiece in the Library came from Wavendon

By 1938, he had made a decision. The house and grounds, with 3,000 acres, should be given to the Trust, which, at that time, owned just six houses and 75,000 acres around the country.

In 1942 the Trust's historic buildings secretary, James Lees-Milne, whose job it was to visit those considering handing their properties to the Trust and to discuss means of doing so, first visited Stourhead. Lees-Milne, who noted his observations in his diaries, published *Ancestral Voices*, his wonderfully candid accounts of these meetings, in 1975. He recollects the eccentric Hoares fondly:

'Sir Henry is an astonishing nineteenth-century John Bull, hobbling on two sticks. He was wearing a pepper and salt suit and a frayed grey billycock over his purple face... Lady Hoare is an absolute treasure, and unique. She is tall, ugly and eighty-two.... She has a protruding square coif of frizzly grey hair in the style of the late nineties, black eyebrows and the thickest spectacle lenses I have ever seen. They are the dearest old couple. I am quite in love with her out-spoken ways and funny old-fashioned dress.'

James Lees-Milne

During the Second World War Sir Henry allowed an airfield to be built on the estate; it was used by the British, Americans, Canadians and New Zealanders between 1941 and 1945. Personnel, including the Grenadier Guards, the 7th Devonshire Regiment and the Liaison Regiment, in which actor David Niven commanded 'A' squadron, stayed in the house and local buildings.

He describes the scene at dinner: '...he spoke very little, and that little addressed to himself. She kept up a lively and not entirely coherent prattle...'.

The following morning Sir Henry took Lees-Milne on the tour around the lake; the Baronet drove in his custom-made electric wheelchair, his guest following: ' ... I gallop at breakneck speed behind him... He keeps saying "Where are you? Why don't you say something?" When I do catch up I am so out of breath I can't get the words out. All he says (to himself) is, "I don't understand what's come over the boy".'

Stourhead was made over to the National Trust in 1946. On Lady Day, 1947, Sir Henry and Lady Alda died within hours of one another. The remaining 2,215 acres of the estate were left to a distant cousin, Henry Peregrine Rennie Hoare (known as Rennie), who moved into Stourhead with his young family.

Stourhead since 1946

Above left Visitors with a baby sitting by the lake at Stourhead, Wiltshire

Below Orchids on Whitesheet Hill

Sir Henry's 'Memorandum of Wishes' asked the National Trust to make provision for a member of the Hoare family to live in the house. Rennie Hoare's young family lived there until 1956, and an apartment is still retained for family use. The Trust was given not only the house and garden but also the 1,072-hectare (2,650-acre) estate of chalk downland, mixed woodland and the best arable land, supporting four farms which continue centuries of agricultural practices.

The immediate priority was the woodland management where dangerous and decrepit trees were cleared to ensure the long-term survival of the rest. In 1953 a tremendous gale felled many beech, oak, sycamore and chestnut, which were cleared and replaced, largely with beech. Historic vistas were researched and reopened, and some of the paths in the Shades (the slopes shaded by trees on either side of the lake) remade. Grants from the Historic Buildings Council in the 1960s enabled the Trust to repair the leaking dams, the Rock Arch and the roof of the Temple of Apollo.

The landscape garden is managed under a conservation plan drawn up in 1978 and sound management recommendations based on historical research. The plan calls for measures to maintain the visual effects sought by Henry Hoare 'the Magnificent' so, for example, the wonderful understorey of laurel has been systematically restored over recent years and is clipped hard to retain the impression of a glossy green carpet out of which the trees appear to float. Replanting should follow precedent and should aim at simplicity rather than striking varieties of colour or shape. Finally the garden around the lake should be allowed to merge gently into the more pastoral character of the wider landscape, thereby blurring the distinction between garden and park, as was the ambition in the eighteenth century.

These principles have enabled Stourhead to change (as every garden must), while retaining the magical, intangible spirit that has made it a paradise on earth for more than two and a half centuries.

Management of the ancient semi-natural woodland of the wider estate is still a priority. Today's tasks include reversion to native hardwoods and caring for notable trees. The Hoare family still run the estate next door, and we work closely with them in our forestry management.

Right Stourhead is home to a breeding population of rare Tree Sparrows

Far right One of Stourhead's resident dormice in a nest box made by volunteers

The woodland and chalkdowns are home to rare species including the Adonis Blue butterfly and tree sparrow. More common are brown hares, skylarks, bluebells and several varieties of orchid. A project to protect and increase numbers of the rare hazel dormouse has placed 183 nest boxes in appropriate sites.

There are many approaches to the wider landscape, and exploration is encouraged through themed walks, such as the Park Hill Camp walk, leading visitors past the Iron Age hill fort with its large external defence and internal ditch and bank. The Whitesheet Hill walk takes in another hill fort from around 500 BC and an adjacent causewayed camp built 5,500 years ago as well as a Second World War memorial. The finest panorama over the estate is to be had from the top of King Alfred's Tower, reached by a spiral staircase of 205 steps.

Within the estate, business partners and tenants continue the working elements and human traditions that keep Stourhead alive. There are two pubs, an art gallery, farm shop and over fifty cottages.

To cater for over 400,000 annual visitors, the Stourhead Visitor Centre was opened in 1995 and the shop, plant centre and award-winning restaurant followed in 2002. In the spirit of continuous and careful management of change, recent restoration projects have included the Pantheon, the Walled Garden greenhouse, Temple of Apollo and Waterwheel.

Sir Henry's gift to the National Trust was motivated by concern for Stourhead's future and his awareness of how special this place is, and he would be gratified by the pleasure Stourhead gives to so many today.

Below Estate cottages near the entrance to the landscape garden

The Hoares of Stourhead
Owners of Stourhead are set in bold

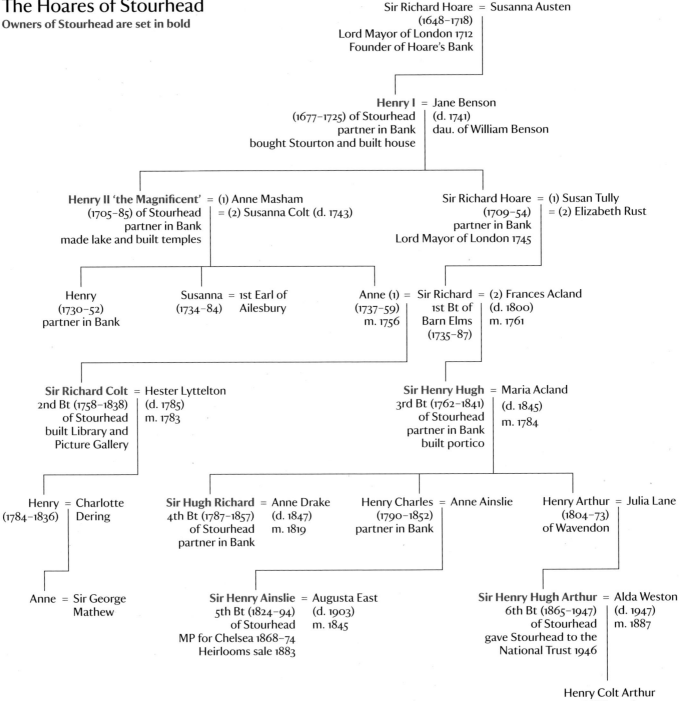

Sir Richard Hoare = Susanna Austen
(1648–1718)
Lord Mayor of London 1712
Founder of Hoare's Bank

Henry I = Jane Benson
(1677–1725) of Stourhead (d. 1741)
partner in Bank dau. of William Benson
bought Stourton and built house

Henry II 'the Magnificent' = (1) Anne Masham
(1705–85) of Stourhead = (2) Susanna Colt (d. 1743)
partner in Bank
made lake and built temples

Sir Richard Hoare = (1) Susan Tully
(1709–54) = (2) Elizabeth Rust
partner in Bank
Lord Mayor of London 1745

Henry
(1730–52)
partner in Bank

Susanna = 1st Earl of
(1734–84) Ailesbury

Anne (1) = Sir Richard = (2) Frances Acland
(1737–59) 1st Bt of (d. 1800)
m. 1756 Barn Elms m. 1761
(1735–87)

Sir Richard Colt = Hester Lyttelton
2nd Bt (1758–1838) (d. 1785)
of Stourhead m. 1783
built Library and
Picture Gallery

Sir Henry Hugh = Maria Acland
3rd Bt (1762–1841) (d. 1845)
of Stourhead m. 1784
partner in Bank
built portico

Henry = Charlotte
(1784–1836) Dering

Sir Hugh Richard = Anne Drake
4th Bt (1787–1857) (d. 1847)
of Stourhead m. 1819
partner in Bank

Henry Charles = Anne Ainslie
(1790–1852)
partner in Bank

Henry Arthur = Julia Lane
(1804–73)
of Wavendon

Anne = Sir George
Mathew

Sir Henry Ainslie = Augusta East
5th Bt (1824–94) (d. 1903)
of Stourhead m. 1845
MP for Chelsea 1868–74
Heirlooms sale 1883

Sir Henry Hugh Arthur = Alda Weston
6th Bt (1865–1947) (d. 1947)
of Stourhead m. 1887
gave Stourhead to the
National Trust 1946

Henry Colt Arthur
(1888–1917)